The Magical Rocking Horse

Written by Matthew Charlton

Sara arrived at Grandma's house. Sara did not like coming on holiday to Grandma's house. Grandma was old and forgetful, and she lived miles and miles from Sara's house and Sara's friends.

This time, Sara wasn't just visiting Grandma for the holidays. She was coming to live with Grandma for a while. Dad was sick, and he had to go into hospital for a while.

"Why can't I stay with Bahira?" Sara asked her father. Bahira was her best friend from school. They did everything together. Now she wouldn't see Bahira until Dad got better and they could go home.

"This can't be Sara?" said an old lady's voice. "My, how you have grown!"
"Hello, Grandma," said Sara.

Grandma welcomed her to the house. It was big and old and had lots of rooms.

"This is your room. It used to be my bedroom, but I can't manage the stairs anymore. So now I sleep next to the kitchen," explained Grandma.

Grandma spent a lot of the day asleep on her chair by the TV, so Sara was alone for much of the day.

At first, she felt lonely and bored. But then she decided to explore the house.

So, the next day, when Grandma fell asleep after lunch, Sara began to poke around. She looked in every room but couldn't find anything interesting. She was about to give up when she pushed against a wooden panel. It creaked and opened to reveal a secret passageway to the attic.

The attic was dark and dusty and full of old boxes. But right at the back, Sara spotted something.

It was an old rocking horse. It was beautiful. It had a white and black-pattered body and a crystal-white mane. Its eyes glowed like polished chestnuts.

"Grandma, you know that old rocking horse in the attic?" said Sara at dinner. "Which old rocking horse?" said Grandma.

How strange, thought Sara to herself. Has Grandma just forgotten? Or did I dream it?

She ran upstairs to double-check. Nope, not dreaming. The rocking horse was definitely real. Too real, almost. Its mane was silky soft. Its eyes sparkled with life. And Sara could swear that it felt warm, even in the cold of the morning.

Sara described the horse again to Grandma, but Grandma insisted she'd never seen it.

"Perhaps it is old Mrs Thingy-ma-jiggy's next door," laughed Grandma. "She must be up to her old tricks."

Old Mrs Thingy-ma-jiggy, or Mrs Thimble, as she was called, was the other reason Sara wasn't bored anymore.

From the upstairs bedrooms, Sara had a clear view of Mrs Thimble's garden. And what a garden it was. It was filled with strange contraptions and cooking equipment.

Mrs Thimble was always sweeping the garden wearing her cloak and pointy hat.

"Grandma," began Sara, "you don't think Mrs Thimble might be a w—"
"A wrinkly old bat?" interrupted Grandma.

"No," Sara tried again, "I mean a w—"
"A wormy old toad?"
"No, a w—"
"A wheezing old crow?"

"Never mind," sighed Sara. It was no use at all talking to Grandma.
She was better off playing on her own.

So every day, Sara played with the rocking horse instead.

Some days, she was riding the winner at the Grand National.

Some days, she was jumping over streams on a cross-country adventure.

And some days, she was a cowgirl herding cattle on the Great Plains.

But Sara just couldn't shake the feeling that there was something special about the rocking horse, something real.

Every day, she watched Mrs Thimble go about her rituals: taking plants from the garden and strange things from pots, cooking them up in her big black pan over the open fire, mumbling as she stirred.

Grandma's and Mrs Thimble's houses stood on the edge of a great forest.

Sara had never been into the forest. Grandma is tired easily, and she couldn't walk that far. And Sara wasn't allowed into the forest on her own.

The closest Sara got to the forest was through the attic window.
She sat up there at dawn, watching the sunrise over the treetops.
She sat there at dusk, watching the birds return home to roost.

And she sat there in the night, when she could not get to sleep, and listened to the forest sing.
For sing it did, every night. A sweet, wordless song.
Sara heard the song, and the rocking horse heard it, too.

"Grandma," Sara asked one morning at breakfast, "do you know any stories about magic around here?"

"Magic?" asked Grandma.
"Anything about the forest singing, or Mrs Thimble, or about the rocking horse in the attic?" said Sara.
"Which rocking horse?" asked Grandma.

Sara sighed. It was hard to talk to her when she forgot everything.

Suddenly, Grandma said, "My great Aunt Myrtle was very superstitious. She taught me an undoing spell. A spell to free a creature trapped in an object. It was simple. Let me see if I can remember it:

"First, take an old key. Then place the key on the forehead of the trapped creature. Finally, say the magic words, 'Prison dweller, you I see; with this key, I set you free'. I think that was it."

The rocking horse! thought Sara. That's it! It's a real horse that Mrs Thimble has cast a spell on!

"But, of course, it's all just nonsense: an old wives' tale," added Grandma.
"Thanks, Grandma!" cried Sara.
"What for?" asked Grandma.

But Sara didn't answer. She was already bounding up the stairs towards the attic, two at a time.

First, Sara took the old brass key from the attic door. Then, she balanced it on the rocking horse's forehead. It was not as easy as it sounded. After three tries, Sara managed to get the key to balance. Finally, she was ready to say the magic words:

"Prison dweller, you I see; with this key, I set you free."

Nothing happened.

Sara's face fell. She had been so certain Grandma's spell would work.
She was about to give up when, suddenly, the rocking horse began to grow.
It got bigger and bigger, and a spiral horn appeared on its forehead.
Sara gazed in wonder. The rocking horse was no more.

Now, in its place, stood a baby unicorn.

The unicorn shook its multicoloured mane, and a shower of stars floated out.

Sara held out her hand. The unicorn sniffed it, came closer, nuzzled her hand.

"There, girl, it's OK," whispered Sara.
The unicorn nuzzled at Sara's pockets.
"Sorry, girl, I don't have anything for you. I'll find you something to eat downstairs."

As they walked downstairs, Sara imagined the look on Bahira's face when she told her all about this.

Grandma didn't seem to find it strange that there was a unicorn in the kitchen. Or if she did, she didn't let on.

"What do unicorns eat?" wondered Sara.
They tried milk, and they tried oats. They tried apples, and they tried bananas. The baby unicorn just shook her head.

"Perhaps we should try something more magical?" suggested Grandma. So they searched the cupboards.

"How about this?" asked Sarah, holding up a tin of starfruit.

The baby unicorn guzzled it in one gulp. Then she curled up under the kitchen table and fell asleep. Sara sat beside her on the floor and stroked her magnificent mane.

"Mrs Thimble must have cast a spell on her and turned her into that rocking horse, that mean old witch," said Grandma. "I was suspicious of that rocking horse from the day it appeared in the attic."

"So you did know about the rocking horse, and you did know Mrs Thimble was a witch!" cried Sara. A thousand questions raced through her head.
    "Where did Mrs Thimble find a unicorn?"
    "The forest, of course," replied Grandma. "Haven't you heard them singing at night?"

"You don't mean that sound is unicorns singing?" asked Sara.
    "Why, of course," continued Grandma, "what else could it be?"

Sara was speechless. At last, she said, "Grandma, why didn't you tell me about any of this magic before?"

Grandma pushed her glasses down her nose and looked straight at Sara.

"Would you have believed me?"

They called the baby unicorn Stardust. For three days, they kept her in the kitchen and fed her tinned starfruit.

And for three days, Grandma told Sara all about her childhood and her life and everything she knew about magic (which was a lot).

For three days, Stardust ate and ate and got bigger and bigger.

"It's like she's making up for all that time stuck in the attic," said Sara.

By the fourth day, Stardust was too big to sleep under the kitchen table.

She was almost too big to fit in the kitchen at all.

That night, as the sun set, Stardust began to sing. And the unicorns in the forest sang back.

"She needs to go back to her family," said Grandma. "It's time."

Sara knew it was true, but it was hard to say goodbye.

They waited until it was pitch black, then they opened the backdoor and led Stardust out into the wood.

They made sure that Mrs Thimble wasn't watching. They didn't want her to catch Stardust and turn her back into a rocking horse.

"Goodbye, friend," said Sara.

Stardust nuzzled Sara's hand for one last time. Then she trotted off into the forest, towards the singing.

Sara opened the hand that Stardust had nuzzled. In it was a plaited twist of Stardust's multicoloured mane. It was a friendship bracelet. She ran her fingers along the loops, and they glowed.

"Thank you, friend," she said out loud.
"I have a feeling that this isn't the last we'll see of Stardust," said Grandma.

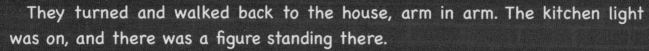

They turned and walked back to the house, arm in arm. The kitchen light was on, and there was a figure standing there.

"Dad!" cried Sara, running to him. "Are you better?"

"Yes, much better," said Dad. "I've come to take you home. Are you ready to go?"

Sara looked at Grandma. Grandma winked at Sara.

"Yes," said Sara, "I'm ready to go home."